THE RAINBOW PENCIL

WRITE AND DRAW JOURNAL

Written by

JESSICA VAUGHT

*For my children,
may this journal encourage and foster
imagination, creative writing, and vivid
illustrations.*

*Every rainbow overcomes the storm.
Create the sunshine.
Be the rainbow.*

JOURNAL PSYCHOLOGY

Writing is a healthy way to express yourself and process your thoughts on paper.

This journal encourages children to express their thoughts and feelings through words, pictures, or both. With repeated use, this journal can become a place where they learn more about themselves, recognize patterns, and process emotions. It can serve as a roadmap for development, helping children and the adults who love them identify strengths and weaknesses and providing a resource for improvement and growth.

Adults, consider writing in your own journal as well. Writing together can create a strong relationship built on trust, love, and support, and when children see adults they love doing something, they are more motivated to do it too.

The pages that follow include positive affirmations for your child to repeat each day and a page with blank space and lines to let their creativity shine. My hope is that this journal brings your child comfort and becomes a positive, safe space to express themselves and explore their feelings, whatever they may be—excited, proud, frustrated, worried, jealous, embarrassed, lonely, etc.

When your child is finished writing in their journal each time, encourage them to share what they wrote about, letting them know that you are there to help in any way you can. It is so important to communicate with your child about the emotions of life in a way the child can relate to. Be honest with them, share your personal experiences in an age-appropriate way. Let them know that it's okay to feel all these emotions and that God has put these emotions in their life to help them grow and develop with each obstacle they may face, overcoming hard times and being resilient.

Be sure to keep this journal in a special place for them to look back on later in life. It may give them the inspiration one day to inspire others, the way my personal journals have for me!

I am a child of God.

I am faithful.

I am loved.

I am valued.

I am beautiful and created with love.

I am courageous and capable of stepping outside of my comfort zone.

I am safe and have
an army of love and support behind me.

I am not afraid of the unknown.
God will always protect me.

I am adventurous and capable of trying new things that interest me.

I am capable of doing hard things.

I am confident and believe in myself.

I am caring. I am kind.

I am honest and
capable of admitting my mistakes.

I am a loyal friend.

I am a hard worker.

I am talented.

I am intelligent.

I am determined.

I am energetic and appreciate fresh air and the outdoors.

I am a leader that others around me look up to.

I am fun to be around.

I am creative in my own special way.

I am imaginative.

I am thoughtful and find joy in making those around me smile.

I am patient and capable
of waiting for my turn.

I am a good listener.

I am capable of taking criticism well to make me stronger.

I am confident in my ability to succeed at what I set my mind to.

I am resilient and capable of building myself back up time and time again.

I stay positive and focus on the bright
side of negative thoughts and emotions.

I am capable of working well with others.

I am dedicated to doing
my best work every day.

I am capable of remaining
calm when upset.

I am empathetic of others' feelings.

I am appreciated for my thoughtful actions.

I am generous and share well with others.

I am worthy of happiness, comfort, and love.

I am compassionate and understanding.

I am respectful to friends, family, and others.

I am responsible for my actions and how I react.

I am capable of forgiving
and moving forward.

I am grateful for everything in my life.

I am creating sunshine by being authentic and genuine.

I am proud to be me.

I am a masterpiece of God.

I am ME.

ABOUT THE AUTHOR

Jessica Vaught is the author of The Rainbow Pencil, which is based on a true story. After losing her grandmother in 2024, she needed to find a way to continue sharing her thoughts, feelings, and dreams with her grandmother. This gave Jessica the encouragement to start her own writing journal in hopes of healing a broken heart and finding the strength to overcome a difficult time in her life.

Through writing, Jessica discovered her true calling—creating children's books as a way to express her gratitude to God and to invite children to recognize their unique gifts.

With strong interests in education, personal development, and continuous growth, Jessica Vaught's passion is to help others acknowledge their full potential and reaffirm the value of each individual. She achieves this mindset by using an out-of-the-box learning approach: going beyond traditional teaching methods, embracing creativity and innovation to engage children, and delivering a more meaningful understanding of the lessons to be learned. She is a firm believer that when there is confidence, there is success. This, in return, leads to a happier mindset, improved engagement, reduced stress, and strong leadership skills.

OTHER BOOKS BY JESSICA

Now available as a coloring book or a full-color illustrated book, *The Rainbow Pencil* tells the story of Valerie, a bright, imaginative girl who sees the world through stories and color.

One rainy day, after seeing a brilliant rainbow in the sky, Valerie dreams up a magical rainbow pencil—one that brings God-given gifts to life with every shade.

The Rainbow Pencil is a heartwarming, faith-filled story that inspires children to embrace their strengths, follow their hearts, and believe in the masterpiece God created them to be. Encouraging self-expression and confidence, this book reminds young readers that their dreams matter, and that every story begins with listening to themselves.

Visit TheRainbowPencil.com to order a coloring book or full-color illustrated book for your child today.

ABOUT PENZIE PRESS

Penzie Press is a strong supporter of childhood mental health advocacy. We are passionate about providing young individuals with life lessons that foster increased motivation, positive thinking, and academic success. Our mission through literature is to encourage children to live a happy and healthy life, building self-esteem, confidence, and acceptance through core values of honesty, empathy, kindness, responsibility, critical thinking, and resilience. We use a neurodiverse friendly font to encourage an enjoyable reading and learning experience for all.

Our mission statement is: "Create the sunshine. Be the rainbow." We believe that when children listen to their hearts, their authentic selves shine brightly through their actions. Our goal is to encourage people to come together, be kind to one another, and accept the differences that make us unique.